SPEYSIDE MEMORIES

Boyhood and Beyond
on River and Hill

Norman Matheson

Matador
9 Priory Business Park,
Wistow Road, Kibworth Beauchamp,
Leicestershire. LE8 0RX
Tel: 0116 279 2299
Email: books@troubador.co.uk
Web: www.troubador.co.uk/matador
Twitter: @matadorbooks

ISBN 978 1838595 449

British Library Cataloguing in Publication Data.
A catalogue record for this book is available from the British Library.

Printed by CPI Group (UK) Ltd, Croydon, CR0 4YY
Typeset in 12pt Sabon by Troubador Publishing Ltd, Leicester, UK

Matador is an imprint of Troubador Publishing Ltd

In memory of the companionship of those close to nature,
ghillies and deerstalkers, who enriched my days on river and hill.

Acknowledgements

I am grateful to Alison Williams for constructive criticism of the layout and for meticulous editorial correction of the manuscript. I also thank my daughter, Fiona, for helpful assistance during the coronavirus lockdown.

Finally, it is a pleasure to acknowledge the cordial efficiency of Fern Bushnell, Production Controller, Troubador Publishing Ltd.

Contents

FOREWORD .... *ix*

AUTUMN PLUNDER 1

ECHOES OF LAUGHTER IN STRATHAVON 11

A MAN FROM SKYE 19

VARIETY: THE SPICE OF FISHING 27

A MEMORABLE FISH FROM ARNDILLY 35

SNOW ON THE WIND 41

ORTON ON SONG 51

A MEMORABLE GHILLIE 55

SALMON STALKED AT TULCHAN 63

ANDREW FOWLER'S REEL 69

A PEARL FROM HEAD OF WOOD 73

Foreword

For those of us, like me, who are the wrong side of our allotted three score years and ten, the recalling of memories of childhood and youth growing up before, during, and after the Second World War becomes increasingly evocative. Here we have a collection of short stories illuminated with watercolour illustrations and images that tell of beautiful places, rivers and streams, remarkable relatives, engaging local characters, dedicated gamekeepers, unforgettable ghillies, and stirring fishing tales of both success and failure.

All are lifelong cherished memories, written as entertaining stories told with nostalgia, occasional emotion, humour, warmth, and charm in abundance. *Speyside Memories* is a worthy companion book to the acclaimed *A Speyside Odyssey* and is a moving tribute to a way of life very distant from that we experience today in the 21st century.

Although the number of our beloved salmon entering our rivers and streams has declined in recent times, the countryside and its many colourful characters so enjoyably described remain largely unchanged, as delightful and welcoming to the visitor to the beautiful Highlands of Scotland as ever. Long may it continue!

David J James   President   The Flyfishers' Club   London   2020

Autumn Plunder

The small corn yard

In upper Banffshire the rowans were red and the late harvest had been gathered in. Stubble fields lay bare and three well-built rucks stood proud like burly sentinels in the small corn yard. Which tells that this tale is from the past. It comes from a time when I was but a boy, not yet conscious of man's inhumanity to man and hardly aware of the devastating blitzkrieg that was sweeping through Europe.

The day's work had ended and porridge was on the kitchen table. Despite the war, food was plentiful: oatmeal, potatoes, milk, churned butter, eggs, rabbits in unlimited numbers and white hares in winter (but preserve me from that dubious delicacy: hare soup). What might be seen as mundane fare was occasionally enlivened by illicit endeavour. Partridges were common in those years though pheasants were less often available. There was no scarcity of grouse, but these were more valued as a source of income. An occasional salmon, however, taken by what was known as the local method, was welcome. Once or twice a year, a hogget was surreptitiously slaughtered. This secretive, primitive and gory deed was not a pretty sight, but the end product might be said to have justified the means.

Although the apparent abundance was more evident at midday, porridge was the usual fare at suppertime. But monotony was relieved by the treat that often followed, a thick wedge of girdle scone, well fired on top and light as a feather. Spread with butter and rhubarb jam, it made for youthful bliss. That my grandmother could conjure up such delights on a black girdle suspended over the peat fire is a testimony to bygone skills. As to jam, rhubarb was common, never strawberry and not often raspberry for there were few wild rasps and none in cultivation. Cranberries were tedious to pick but the tart flavour of the excellent jam lives in my memory. Though seldom available, jam made from those wonderful berries, known locally as averons (cloudberries) was unique. Above two thousand feet, averons are not uncommon but in flower they are susceptible to spring frosts and years may pass without fruit. During the same year as the event about to unfold took place, Alick Elder, the local gamekeeper, looked in past, as he customarily did, though never apparently in a covert search for ill-gotten game. Nonetheless, it was wise to be vigilant: a brace of birds hanging on the back of the kitchen door was best quickly removed. Eck, as he was known, regularly patrolled the high tops and announced that there was a good crop of averons. Given directions, I was sent off with a basket, to cross the burn and struggle through waist-high heather before reaching easier higher ground, then ever on and upwards until the smallholding stood out in miniature, far below. The expanse of characteristic foliage came in sight and the basket was soon filled with large ripe yellow berries. I contrived to deliver them safely, without having stumbled and tipped them out on the descent. And jam was made. However, I now know that averons, a delicacy in Scandinavia, are most delicious when simply mixed with sugar and whipped cream.

By the time I was tackling the scone, my antennae were alerted to something unnatural in the behaviour of three men at the table: my Uncle Donald, The Duke and Tom. Donald, who farmed the smallholding, was characterised by his mischievous sense of humour. Little could pass him by without an excuse for ridicule, fun and laughter, which, if at times somewhat strained, was lightsome and infectious. The Duke, who helped out with the farm work, was tall and well built but the origin of his nickname was obscure: he certainly bore no resemblance either in appearance, bearing or diction to the aristocracy. Tom, the "fee't loon" (young farm worker), was small in stature but well muscled. As the local highland games drew near, Tom fancied his chances as a budding heavy athlete, at least in the local events. In the summer evenings there were nightly gatherings for practice and light-hearted competition amongst neighbouring contenders. Tom excelled in throwing the twenty-eight pound weight and was hard to beat in putting the light stone, but wrestling was his downfall. Regularly challenged by my Auntie Madge and egged on by my father, who would enticingly place a pound note under a stone as the prize for the winner of the contest, Tom should have known better than to have accepted those challenges. Madge was always the winner, deploying her considerable weight to advantage by grabbing hold of the slighter Tom and contriving to fall on top of him. Tom could only struggle out from under her vast bulk, winded, deflated and defeated, to watch the ceremonial presentation of the prize money to the inevitable victor. I feel sure of collusion between Madge and my father since I cannot imagine him willing to part with a pound on such patent frivolity.

As the table was cleared, my subliminal suspicions persisted but were set aside when I was sent out into the stillness of the gloaming to shut up the hen house. A fox in a hen house is to be avoided at all costs. The fox might be forgiven if it took sufficient only for its immediate needs. But, not so, it will delight in slaughtering every hen down to the last one, a disaster marked by a raucous din of frantic squawking and clouds of feathers as panic-stricken hens burst into the air in a vain bid to escape the inevitable snap of the lethally efficient jaws.

The hens safely shut in, I lingered on in the silence of the fugitive day. Then I heard it. And heard it again, from the moss-hag where the bog myrtle grew, that weird and forlorn sound of the uplands, the drumming of a snipe. It is difficult to explain the emotive effect of such plaintive sounds. The bubbling call of the whaup (curlew) is in the same poignant vein while the bleating of the Golden Plover on high ground may be the most evocative of all. These mournful sounds of the heath, breaking the silence, are definitely melancholy and yet, in a way strangely comforting, awakening in an impressionable mind a sense of belonging, of being in tune with the spirit of the land, at one with nature and the remote loneliness of wilderness.

A sudden shaft of light streaming from the back door interrupted my youthful reverie. The trio emerged, striding purposefully across the green, past the peat stack towards the road. I hurried to catch up, only to be discouraged with a surly dismissal.

"Awa' hame noo, you're nae comin' wi' us!"
"Why no? Whar are ye goin'?"
"Niver you mind, awa' ye go!"

"Whar are ye goin'?"

Dejected, though still in hope, I tagged on, straggling some distance behind. The disparate procession marched on in silence for a good way before I heard more charitable words: "Ach, let the loon come, he micht come in handy." Persistence rewarded, I caught up with relieved anticipation. They carried nothing with them, except for a gwaana bag (jute sack) rolled up under The Duke's arm. On we went in the darkness, past the larger farm and steading, up the incline beneath the overhanging birches, down the brae past the small dwelling in which my grandparents had raised thirteen children, to reach the swing bridge. About a mile had been covered as we crossed the bridge, which, with three adults and a youngster aboard, lived up to its name. Intent still undisclosed, we waded through the long grass, climbing up the field on the far side, and crossing the road as the Church of Scotland manse on its elevated site came into view. Progress was slow, circuitous and cautious, with concealment from undergrowth and bushes evidently necessary as we approached the back of the manse overlooking the large garden. All was in silence and in darkness. As we crouched there, Donald whispered to The Duke to make his way cautiously round to the front of the house to reconnoitre the lie of the land. Minutes passed before we were alerted by the soft rustle of his returning footsteps. Laughter was suppressed as he gleefully announced, "Ach it's a' richt, the minister 's feedin' the bairn."

"The minister's feedin' the bairn"

This homely domesticity he had seen through one of the large front windows. Why this image of the minister, disrobed but with dog collar still on, nursing the infant, should have caused amusement is not easy to say. It may have had something to do with the minister's personality, well-meaning, gentle, and kind, but vulnerable and especially vulnerable to the admittedly rather infantile humour that so prevalently poked fun at those who strayed beyond the phlegmatic norm.

This reassuring news was the signal for brisk activity as the raiding party clambered over the garden wall to reach the Victoria Plum tree. I received a command, "Get up that tree, loon, and shak the branches as hard as ye can." Ever ready to climb a tree, I was soon up and shaking the branches. The ripe plums came raining down. The bag was unfurled and, with ever a backward glance at the still dark aspect of the manse, the plums were rapidly gathered up.

When a halt was called, the bag appeared to be half full. Considering that it was a half-hundredweight sack, it must have by then contained some twenty pounds or more of the forbidden fruit. Much later it occurred to me that there must have been preliminary reconnaissance. Otherwise, how was the size of the crop, as well as its ripeness, sufficiently well known to have justified the well-timed venture?

Our nefarious deed, transacted with no trace of sympathy for the hapless minister, appeared to have been accomplished without incident and we triumphantly retraced our steps. As the bridge came in sight however, our jocular progress came to an abrupt halt. On the far side, just perceptible through the darkness, we could, with immediate concern, make out a tall figure pacing to and fro, thereby cutting off our retreat. "Oh my God," I heard, "I bet the minister's seen us and phoned the bobby!" As we lay concealed in the long grass, it seemed an unwelcome probability, destined to bring our light-hearted bravado to a sticky end. As time passed apprehension persisted. Then the apparition changed tactics. His pacing vigil ceased. We strained our eyes but he was definitely no longer visible. Presumably he was lying in wait. Ultimately, patience expired and, by way of investigation, Tom, the slightest in bulk, apart from me who would not have been deemed up to the task, was despatched to crawl across the bridge, making himself as near to invisible as possible. With limited choice and in pitch darkness, the chance of getting away with this dubious assignment seemed worth the risk. Off he went. We could scarcely make out the prone figure inching its way over the bridge until lost from sight. Time hung heavily before Tom reappeared, striding boldly back towards our lair. On hearing his report, spirits rose: "Ach, it's only Eck Elder an' he's lyin' deid-drunk in the ditch, his bike on top o' 'im." Confidence restored and mightily relieved, we hurried across the bridge and, in passing, gave a fond and sympathetic salute to the snoring miscreant. Eck was renowned for his unconstrained liaisons with the bottle. It was as well that these trysts were infrequent, limited as they were by his modest means, for he never came off the better of them. In the colder light of day, more dispassionate reflection would have put the fictitious bobby down to a figment of fertile imagination, for the good minister would surely never have stooped to such a low-minded course of action.

We stepped out jauntily for home and I, privileged to be included in what seemed in conclusion to have been an exciting and productive adult venture, had grown in stature. More sober beings would have pronounced our conduct lamentable, which it admittedly was. No doubt it had been hatched as an adventurous ploy to lighten the daily darg, heightened by an element of risk, in which the bounty was a minor attraction. The minister's vulnerable nature was likely to have been additionally inviting, a factor certain to add to opprobrium in the eyes of the unco-guid. In defence, it might be stoutly asserted that there were still plenty of plums left on the tree. Furthermore, the exploit might be claimed to have been of tangible benefit to the parish in that during the following week or two, plums, source perhaps suspected but unrevealed, were generously distributed amongst the locals.

Within days of our dark deed, the minister, gentle soul that he was, called in to visit my grandmother. As he sat opposite her at the peat fire, sipping his tea and voicing the platitudes of his calling, I took advantage of an opportunity of discomfiting my uncle in repayment for his frequent practical jokes and ridiculing of me. We were at the table, a little distance away, my uncle sheltering behind the Press & Journal and taking no part in the pastoral scene, when I questioned, *sotto voce*, whether it would not be a kindness to offer the minister a small bag of plums. Though more than seventy years have passed, I can still see the startled look on his face for it would not have been beyond me to have carried out the threat.

Any plums for the minister?

Echoes of Laughter
in Strathavon

Life as a boy during the war (1939-1945) on a small farm in upper Banffshire may appear to have been somewhat austere. In terms of utilities, the solitary tap, delivering a hesitant stream of cold water, was the sole convenience. There was no hot water, wash hand basin, bathroom or toilet. The outdoor shack in a nearby field, which served as a toilet for those prepared to tolerate its ambience, was not entirely noxious. The strong scent from sun-baked resin in its knotty planks did much to counteract its less agreeable odour. And gaps in its walls permitted contemplative observation of any surrounding activity. Alternatively, secluded sites *en plein air* were freely available for the more discerning.

There was of course no electricity, radio, television or telephone. The torpid silence of a Sunday afternoon was broken only by the insistent ticking of the wag at the wa'. At night the ubiquitous hissing Tilley lamp gave adequate light in the kitchen (living area) but I went to bed carrying a candle. Once in bed however, with the skylight open, the musical hush and gurgle of the nearby burn was memorably enchanting.

During the winter months, as a consequence of the lack of any source of heat other than the peat fire, chilblains were inevitable. However, the intolerable itch was less distressing than the agony of the recommended treatment. The advice was to run bare-foot in the snow, round and round the peat stack, until all sensation in the feet had gone. This wretched cure could hardly have been more irrational and, I feel sure, detrimental.

Food was largely dependent on oatmeal, potatoes and milk. Porridge twice a day and potatoes and milk as a main course once a week was customary. Rabbit, cooked in various ways was the most common source of meat. Oatcakes, made with consummate skill on a large black girdle hanging on the swey over the peat fire, were on the table at every meal together with home made butter, crowdie and a basin of milk. As a regular treat, girdle scones, large and light, were baked on the same surface. This simple fare was nonetheless enjoyable and never in short supply.

However, even had there been any sense of deprivation, it would have been transcended by mirth. Little was required as an excuse for light-hearted humour. Admittedly, the irrepressible comedy was often strained and overworked but it still provoked laughter. Imitation of the behaviour of individuals who strayed from the norm was a common source of mischievous amusement. In terms of bizarre speech or outlandish pronouncements, two men come to mind. Charlie Spalding in his baker's van had the curious affectation of expressing himself mainly on inspiration. The pitch of his sentences would rise with increasing sibilant intake until expiration was inevitable. His curious diction lent itself to gentle parody and, when poised at his counter with a penny or two for sugary confections, laughter had to be suppressed.

The kenspeckle Eck Elder, an archetypal Scottish gamekeeper who might be spied covering ground on East Cromdale shortly after first light, was another source of mild ridicule. Eck was from the borders and retained the strong accent of his youth. His complaint, 'flaks as big as pat lids' (flakes as big as pot lids) in deploring a severe snowstorm was but one of his colourful pronouncements that invited imitation.

But surpassing such modest sources of fun, when fun of any kind had to be home made, was the remarkable Willie McGillivray. Willie, tall and gaunt, was a water bailiff who patrolled the A'en (Avon) between Tomintoul and Glenlivet. He lived in one of a few houses on the secluded slopes at the top of Glenlochy, reached by a side road near the Bridge of Brown. Daily he traversed the 'double bend' as he called it, on a motor bike, his invariable form of transport. Willie was seldom seen other than astride his highly esteemed Indian motor-bike and usually with the engine still running even when stationery, which no doubt gave invaluable audible warning to poachers on the water. Willie had a curiously fertile imagination in that his rather simple stories, told with serious drama in his lilting highland accent, were, with one notable exception, patent nonsense. Three of his stories are given below.

A Resourceful Hen

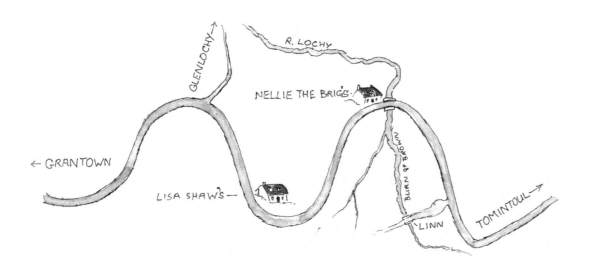

Map of the 'Double bend'

"Man, I was coming down the double bend the other day and as I came in sight o' Lisa Shaw's, I saw a brown hen sitting at the roadside. When I passed by, damn me, she flew up on to the tank o' the bike. I carried on down the brae with my bold passenger but, when I got the length o' Nellie the Brig's, the hen flew off. I thought nothing more about it and went on to Tomintoul for the messages. But on the way home, there was the hennie sitting at the roadside at Nellie the Brig's waiting for a lift back."

A Cow in Distress

"When I was on Lochyside yesterday I saw there was something far wrong wi' a cow in the field by the roadside. It was aye twitch, twitch, twitchin' its head. I went over to the fence and then I saw what was wrong: there was a straw sticking out o' the cow's lug. Ach lassie, says I, come here and I'll soon relieve you. Well, well, I reached out and pulled out the straw but what do you think? Out flew a starling. Then he added, by way of needless explanation, "It had built its nest in the cow's lug."

Wayward Salmon

"What a fine surprise I got this morning. When I looked round my snares I couldn't believe what I'd caught: there was six salmon in them."

The implication that salmon, in an urge to reach their spawning ground, had taken a short cut over dry land suggested that Willie's imagination had reached a zenith of absurdity. Not so, however. On this occasion he was justifiably perplexed: there were in fact six salmon in his snares. I could name the individuals responsible for what, considering Willie's propensities as well as his occupation, was an imaginative practical joke.

At the back end in those years the tributaries of the A'en were full of fish and, at the dead of night with a lamp and gaff, a large number could readily be taken out. But it required keen sense of humour to overlook the inconvenience of transporting six fish from the River Lochy to Willie's distant snares. Lest there be doubters, many boxes of salmon caught by lamp and gaff used to go by train from the Braes of Glenlivet to Billingsgate. Such illegal bounty, in addition to the large consignments of grouse sent south, made a welcome contribution to a thin existence. Perhaps such covert exploits are still part of the way of life in those remote glens, but who knows?

Sadly, Willie McGillivray died of tuberculosis in his forties. However, his stories live on and, when driving down the double bend and pausing as always to gaze in wonder at the Linn of Brown, I fancy that I may see a brown hen waiting by the roadside at Nellie the Brig's.

A Man from Skye

My paternal grandfather, Donald Matheson, who came from the Isle of Skye, must have been a kenspeckle figure in A'enside (Avonside). Bearded and pipe smoking, he retained the lilt of his youthful west highland accent and would occasionally lapse into Gaelic. His father came from the small farm of Aird, the most northern habitation on the island, but he was raised as a boy in Balmaqueen on the south side of Kilmaluag bay. In the sketch of Kilmaluag Bay, the distant building is Aird and the nearer one, Lower Aird, now named Aird Cottage.

Kilmaluag Bay, Aird and Lower Aird

Improbable though it may seem, he left Skye at the age of thirteen to make his way on the mainland. He accompanied a few men driving a flock of sheep to upper Banffshire, where he spent the rest of his life as a shepherd, initially at the Lettoch farm in the Braes of Glenlivet and later for many years on the Delnabo Estate near Tomintoul. During the remainder of his life, when I came to know him, his home was at the Milton, a smallholding in A'enside (Avonside) on the left bank of the River A'en some five miles downstream of Tomintoul.

The Milton from the right bank of A'en

My grandfather married a younger woman from the Braes of Glenlivet and fathered thirteen children, two of whom led distinguished careers in Alberta in Canada. Although, he was said to have gone to school, erratically I suspect, he could neither read nor write. A nightly ritual I witnessed, in front of the peat fire in the Milton, was my grandmother's reading aloud the detailed content of the daily Press and Journal, page after page, as he reclined attentively in a cloud of pipe smoke.

The nightly ritual

Although the Milton, mainly a sheep farm, was farmed by my Uncle Donald, my grandfather still took a hand with the hirsel of Black Faced and Cross Bred Cheviot sheep. His own dog, an Old English Sheepdog, with eyes peering through a curtain of hair, stood out amongst the ubiquitous Border Collies. Surprisingly, it rejoiced in the curious name of Bonzo, which I suspect to have been an inspiration of my uncle's irrepressible sense of humour. The dog was also remarkable in its comprehension of the Gaelic language, in which it was spoken to, commanded, and at times reprimanded, with voluble Gaelic invective. These enraged outbursts were inevitably a source of much fun and frequent mimicry by minors such as me.

Gaelic invective

However, we heard the language of my grandfather's youth in a more sensitive way during occasional evenings when he would lapse into poignant Gaelic love songs of which he seemed to have a surprising repertoire, considering that he left Skye at thirteen. Unfortunately his renditions struggled to find much tunefulness, a feature that kindled our unkindly and poorly concealed amusement. We should have appreciated with some sensitivity the touching way in which an old man sought to revive in emotive song the distant memories of the island of his birth.

My grandfather, aged 87, lay terminally ill during the harsh winter of 1942. For the last two weeks of his life he spoke only Gaelic, which was distressing for his relatives who had no understanding of what he was trying to communicate. In 1942, when I lived with my parents in Glenlivet, I remember that, night after night, my father walked from Glenlivet to the Milton and back, a total distance of some ten miles (16km), through the deep snow that blanketed the upper Speyside glens, to see his father who lay close to death. This challenging discharge of duty, had that been its motivation, or, had it been a heartfelt expression of love, was to me as a boy quite remarkable and still is.

My grandfather's death occasioned one of the most memorable journeys of my lifetime. My parents, together with my father's sister Jessie, who was temporarily staying with us in Glenlivet, and me, aged ten, travelled to A'enside on the night before the funeral by horse and sledge. In the deep snow of one of the most severe winters in living memory, no other means of transport was possible. All minor roads were blocked and vehicular traffic was at a standstill for weeks on end.

The romantic overtones of the journey would certainly have been enhanced had we improbably luxuriated in a Russian troika drawn by a team of three and with a tinkling bell above to sound our joyful approach. There were no such refinements, but the sledge bore a large platform, perfectly adequate for two generously proportioned women and a boy squeezed between the two, covered in all the travelling rugs that could be found and with hot water bottles providing transient warmth at the outset. The seating area was elevated above substantial steel runners and the sledge was drawn by a single horse, led by my father, who of course was familiar with the route and could identify the location of the roadway, obscured though it was by deep and drifted snow.

We set off in the dark, although the unremitting pristine blanket of white reflected what light there was. I have no clear memory of the more open sections of the road beyond Drumin Farm, where drifting snow must have been deep. However, decidedly memorable was our progress from then onwards, through tunnels of overarching birch trees, as we made steady progress through A'enside. Occasionally the branches of a birch, stirred by a breath of wind, would release a mound of snow on to our semirecumbent forms but, on the whole, the sledge journey was comfortable. And, more memorably, I at least was absorbed by the romantic overtones of this very unusual form of transport.

When we finally arrived at the Milton the house must have been full of relatives and I recall sharing a bed with my father. My memory of the following morning is of the coffin on a smaller horse-drawn sledge sliding gracefully over the packed snow from the back door of the house, past the peat stack to reach the minor road from Tomintoul to Glenlivet. This road, which in common with all roads in the area was completely impassable except by foot or by horse, led downstream to cross the A'en at what in these years was known as the 'red brig'. Thereafter the coffin would have continued upstream to the Kirkmichael graveyard where so many of my relatives lie and where I now never pass without reflectively wandering amongst so many well known graves.

Considering my age, it was natural that I was not included in the small party that bravely followed the coffin on its snow bound journey from the Milton to the graveyard, a distance of around two miles (3km). As I stood somewhat solemnly watching, I witnessed the most poignant sight of the occasion, my grandmother weeping uncontrollably at the door of their modest dwelling. I imagined her distress to have been at the disappearing sight of her companion of so many years, an expression that might genuinely have been a sentiment of profound and heartfelt love. However, I understood later that she was mainly distressed by what she perceived as the unforgivable slight of the final journey to his grave being on a sledge rather than by a more dignified and fitting form of transport. My immature emotions were different. The departure of the coffin, sliding gracefully on its snow-bound final journey from home, seemed to me to represent an elegant and entirely appropriate motion of farewell. It certainly created an indelible image of my grandfather's end of life that lives on vividly in my memory.

Variety: The Spice of Fishing

I was introduced to fishing at the improbable age of three. My kindly and amusing uncle would take me to one of the nearby pools on the Milton Burn and cast in a worm. Once he was confident of having hooked a small brown trout, he would immediately hand me the rod to "have a go". No sooner had I the rod in my hand, than I felt the exciting wriggle. I had, to my surprise and delight, "caught a fish", and evidently all down to my own emergent skill.

The Milton Burn, which played a significant role in my love of nature, flowed but a matter of yards from the back door of my grandfather's smallholding, the Milton, situated on the left bank of the river A'en (Avon) some five miles (8 km) downstream of Tomintoul. Apart from the convenience of an endless number of small pools within walking distance, in which brown trout were readily caught, the magical song of the burn, a constant murmur and gurgle, audible through the open skylight of my tiny bedroom, lulled me nightly to contented sleep.

As a child and usually alone, I didn't venture into the upper reaches of the burn beneath the distant Blue Rocks, which were predictably alleged to house trout of remarkable size. This claim I was inclined to doubt, an opinion perhaps coloured by reluctance to stray too far into unfamiliar heights. But the lower reaches of the burn had its own charm, especially the expanse of bog myrtle (Myrica gale) rightly celebrated for its aromatic resinous scent. Ever since my youth I never miss the opportunity of crushing a sprig of bog myrtle to release its evocative aroma, thus reviving the long gone days of highland childhood.

On the margins of the boggy ground there was also the understated beauty of damp-loving wild flowers, the occasional nodding deep blue trumpets of common butterwort (Pinguicula vulgaris) fascinating for its insectivorous properties, and the sulphur yellow spires of bog asphodel (Narthecium ossifragrum). Wandering up and down the Milton burn, a basket, had I owned such an elegant angling accoutrement, would have been readily filled with small brown trout. And a sizzling frying pan full of oatmeal coated tiny trout nestling together made a pretty and appetising sight.

However, as a product of upper Speyside, I naturally graduated to larger fish and to larger waters, the River Livet to begin with and later to the Ballindalloch water of the A'en. As a teenager on Livet and A'en, worm remained the most popular bait. Very effective it was, but more skill than may have been readily appreciated was necessary in its deployment. More mature years led to competence in salmon fishing and especially in regular fly-fishing on most beats of Spey and the Aberdeenshire Dee as well as on other rivers.

A lifetime's absorption with fishing and with its attendant closeness to nature led to interest further afield, in which the origin of my grandfather in the Isle of Skye played a significant role. The familial association with Skye included regular contact with remaining Matheson relatives in the north of the island, some of them still living on my great-grandfather's small farm of Aird, the most northern habitation on the island. It was natural that I developed a sense of affinity with the Isle of Skye, and especially with the township of Kilmaluag. Driving from Portree through the dramatic landscape of the eastern route, the unfolding panorama of Kilmaluag bay came to engender a definite sense of belonging. This attachment was based on the sights and sounds of landscape, seascape, atmosphere and personalities as well as on memories. Apart from these sentiments, I became captivated by fishing of a different type: for years after I was introduced to it, sea fishing from the rocks and by boat became addictive.

I was first taken to the island in 1944 at the age of twelve. My father and I stayed at Aird with Seumas, whom I looked on as an uncle, his sister Chrissie and cousin Flora. Aside from the fun of my insatiable attempts to speak the language, coached and teased by the irrepressible Flora, there were novel features of the way of life. The furniture gave little away in terms of comfort: all seating was in the form of basic wooden chairs. And long lines of drying fish were suspended on high, wall to wall across the living area. Finally, soon after we had retired upstairs to bed, we were intrigued by audible low-pitched vocal droning, percolating upwards from below. In time we identified this as the nightly ritual of family worship. The sonorous sounds of devotion sent us to sleep in the same way that the musical hush and gurgle of the Milton Burn lulled me as a boy.

During following years, occasional visits to Skye were memorable. Apart from the dominant sea in its various moods, the warmth of kinship and the subliminal sense of homecoming, sea fishing became an additional passion. Years ago fishing made a significant contribution to crofting subsistence but now the inshore population of fish is markedly depleted and, although it is not the only factor, sea fishing as an integral part of the crofting way of life appears to have become insignificant.

In the mid 1950s my future wife and I were on holiday in the west and decided to divert unannounced to Kilmaluag, hopeful of a day or two's fishing. Once settled into Flora MacDonald's Cottage, still part of the Flodigarry Hotel, we drove the short distance towards Kilmaluag. As the bay came into sight, we saw three distant figures walking down the incline towards us. As they approached, it became clear that these were my relatives, Seumas, Chrissie and Flora, all clad in black and carrying bibles. Once the clamour of our warm welcome abated, I brightly announced that we were looking forward to some fishing.

Three relatives approaching

Seumas' response was an unexpected revelation.

"Och no Norman, there'll be no fishing this week, no fishing at all. It is communion week."

Communion week! We had never known of such an alien prolonged religious imposition, evidently destined to crack down on secular pursuits perceived to be ungodly. Although dismayed, we parted company amicably and returned deflated to Flodigarry Hotel, where we sought solace in the bar. The barman being a genial sort, I could hardly resist soliciting his commiseration.

"Ach yes," says he, "that's right enough, it is communion in Kilmuir. But it's no communion in Staffin!"

The district of Staffin was dispersed immediately to the south of the hotel and several habitations in the Staffin townships were visible from where we stood. The barman pointed out a distant low dwelling.

"If you go down to the croft there and speak to Donald-John, he'll take you out."

Although confidence in this inviting proposal would have been premature, our hopes were definitely raised.

The next morning I knocked on the door of Donald-John's modest dwelling and was received shyly by his wife, comely, rosy-cheeked and clad in an enveloping flowery apron. She listened to my tentative request and answered with a meaningful sigh:

"Well, well, Donald-John is scything hay, but if he hears any word of fishing, the scythe will be thrown aside."

And so it proved to be. Donald-John would have been in his late forties, tall and broad-shouldered, warm-hearted, soft spoken though taciturn and he was obviously every bit as keen to take out a boat as we were to be indulged. But first we had to go to the western side of the island to gather mussels for bait. There were few mussels on the eastern side, at least in the north and we often made do with limpets, which were inferior as bait as well as much less convenient to use. The rowing boat was launched into the sea swell of Staffin Bay and Donald-John took the oars. As we rowed across the featureless expanse of the bay he insightfully predicted the location of the haddock bed and we lowered our hand lines. These bore a terminal crosspiece of wire with lengths of nylon and baited hooks suspended at either end. It was thus possible to catch two fish at one time.

Fishing was astonishingly productive. I could never have envisaged such an abundance of handsome large haddock accumulating steadily in the well of the boat. Ultimately, on the grounds of safety, it would have been foolhardy to take any more aboard. Somewhat reluctantly a halt was called and Donald-John pulled manfully for the shore. This uniquely productive experience was overwhelming but above all we were captivated by the kindness, competence and companionship of our new-found friend.

But, what were we to do with all these fish, something to which we had given no thought? We modestly selected two, proposing to have them served for breakfast at Flodigarry the next morning. Otherwise, the only solution for the bulk of the catch appeared to depend on a possibility of selling it in Portree. With the car overloaded with a total of seven boxes of prime haddock and bumping up and down on the uneven road, we drove to Portree where Donald-John transacted their sale for a sum that appeared to be little more than a pittance. In addition, as I could have confidently predicted, he adamantly refused any kind of reward from us for the time, effort and skill he gave so generously and light-heartedly.

Although the joys of sea fishing later gave way to the more challenging and absorbing pursuit of salmon on Spey and Dee in particular, of such experiences and of such men indelible memories remain.

A Memorable Fish from Arndilly

On a Monday morning in March 1981, I, now a consultant surgeon, was lying comfortably in bed when the telephone rang. A general practitioner acquaintance of mine in Aberlour, told me that he was with a patient, Mrs Samuel of Arndilly. He felt sure she had appendicitis and asked if I would be able to undertake her care. My heart fell since I had arranged a week's leave and a commitment to look after the patient would put paid to any such arrangement. When I expressed hesitation to become involved, he responded, "Aye, maybe so, but it is Mrs Samuel of Arndilly". Despite the inconvenience, I felt obliged to help my friend and agreed to admit the patient immediately.

Mrs Samuel did in fact have appendicitis. The operation was straightforward and, as a matter of courtesy, I rang the GP in the evening to confirm the accuracy of his diagnosis. His immediate response was. "Aye, aye but ye see I was in the big hoose and wisna able to speak freely. But this is Mrs Samuel of Arndilly. You are bound to get fishing!" So, my GP friend was doing his best to accommodate my well-known interest in salmon fishing.

During Mrs Samuel's convalescence, I met her husband, the Hon Mr Tony Samuel, who at that time was the owner of the famous Arndilly beat on Spey. Having been told of my interest in fishing, he kindly invited me to fish his own rod for a day on Arndilly, during which he insisted that he would be my ghillie, a proposition I received with mixed emotion. The appointed day, 22nd April 1981, was during prime time, although the season had been poor. Unfortunately, the weather was bitterly cold with regular snow showers and a strong wind, gusting upstream and across, into the right bank, which made casting very difficult. The air temperature was 34F(1.1C) and the water 44F(6.7C). The water height, at two inches on the gauge, was very low.

Tail of Long Pool, Arndilly

In the afternoon, I was allocated the Long Pool. The right bank of this dauntingly long pool belongs to Arndilly. I struggled to get out a sunk line while Mr Samuel bravely kept station almost at my elbow for most of the afternoon. By the time I was at the tail of the pool, I abandoned the fly in favour of the spinning rod, which made casting slightly easier, though hardly more effective. About four o'clock Mr Samuel said that he was going up to the house for tea and that I was welcome to join him. However, I was equally free to continue fishing, if so inclined. I opted to continue for a time and was glad to fish on unattended. Mr Samuel wished me well with a request to come up to the house at the end of the day.

I was using a fairly light 2¾ inch wooden minnow and at 5.55p.m. hooked a large fish close to the far bank. Considering the inclement weather, I must have been remarkably keen to carry on for so long after my host had gone. My hands were so numb with cold that I had no feeling in my thumb when controlling the tension on the multiplying reel. However, the fish, which spent most of the time splashing a few feet from the far bank, did not take long to land. I was soon able to lead it through the shallower water across which I had waded and finally on to the bank at 6.07pm. Normally, I would not have recorded these timings accurately, but for the fact that I had suspected the fish to be unusually large. Once the fish was killed, I tried to weigh it on a spring balance but the light had gone to a degree that the scale was scarcely visible. However, I could see that it was over thirty pounds. That a fish of that size took only twelve minutes to land, was down to the wonderful efficiency of the multiplier (a type of spinning reel with a revolving spool), which happens to be an additional benefit in dealing expeditiously with kelts (salmon having spawned the previous year and returning in poor condition downstream).

I proceeded to report to Mr Samuel. When he heard that I had caught a fish of over thirty pounds, he was almost speechless and demanded, "Send for MacDonald!" Jock MacDonald, the head ghillie, shortly appeared and weighed the fish at thirty-six pounds (16 kg), a fresh run cock with a few sea-lice on its head.

Thirty-six pounds!

"It is unfortunate," pronounced Mr Samuel, "that those who catch a fish of over 30 pounds, always seem to be big men. You see, we have a tradition that they receive a length of Arndilly tweed." I had mixed feelings about the tweed since the Arndilly pattern of those years was of dubious attraction, being a small black and white check. Nevertheless, I began to ruminate that a fisherman wearing such an Arndilly jacket would have an interesting story to tell.

After having been given something to eat, I received a cordial farewell and departed in the darkness of the stormy night. As a matter of interest, I had had a successful early season in 1981, having already landed nineteen fish including a fish weighing thirty-one pounds, caught on 6th February at Park on the Aberdeenshire Dee.

Snow on the Wind

He drove onwards in the darkness of the early mid-October morning. As the empty road led into remote uplands, the blush of dawn stole over distant eastern ridges. By daylight, he had reached his isolated destination where the stalker stood in wait at their predetermined rendezvous. Though a generation apart they were kindred spirits, hefted to the high land of their birth. Their relationship was characteristic of the empathy that exists between a deerstalker and the 'rifle', one of the most absorbing pleasures of deer stalking.

The pony had earlier been led away on the long climb to reach its agreed location. They boarded the Land Rover taking the rough road through the lower reach of the glen. The glow of autumn was on the landscape. The high tops were shrouded in mist, but the day promised to be fair: the moderate north wind and increasing warmth of the day should see it lift. They dismounted and took the steep path to the spying point. The stillness was broken only by the crunch of their footsteps and by the murmur of the burn below. With binoculars raised, the vast expanse of the eastern corrie was scanned. Their silent spying was soon enlivened by a far distant sound, the roar of a stag. Roar does not quite capture this haunting and evocative sound of the rut, the deep-throated moaning bellow of a challenging stag. It sets the blood of hill men coursing and was music to their ears.

As expected, there were deer on the opposing hill face, twenty or thirty hinds at a low level accompanied by a good-looking stag. A larger group grazed higher up and further away beneath the skyline. Even with the drawn telescope (a telescope provides higher magnification for assessment in detail), the nearer group was too distant to be sure of the quality of the stag, in terms of size, age and head (antlers). A decision on the stalk would have to wait but the day could now be planned. The wind direction was down through the corrie but concern over approaching on a side wind was dispelled by the reassurance that a north wind always swept upwards on the far face. Although some liberty may be taken with their visual acuity, there can certainly be no liberty with the red deer's acute sense of smell. Fortunately, either group could be approached from above. Wind direction permitting, it is ideal to stalk from above. Even the most alert old hind is disinclined to watch the higher ground.

They retreated from the spying point to make the necessary long detour out of sight on low ground. They would then climb beyond the ridge to come in over the skyline directly above the lower group of hinds. Five 130grain bullets were pressed into the revolving magazine of the .270 Mannlicher and the bolt closed on the empty barrel, a measure of absolute safety. Towards midday they crested the skyline and continued to lose height, watchful against coming into the sight of the higher group, to reach a point from which the main stag could be spied. Restless, in the heat of the rut, and intent on dismissing smaller intruding stags, the master, several hundred yards away, was in his prime, large-bodied and with a well-proportioned ten-point head. Although it would have been possible to stalk within range, there was no question of shooting such a stag.

They withdrew, climbing back to the skyline and beyond it to approach the higher lot. The high location of these deer, together with deep peat hags above them, promised a relatively easy approach, provided the final position would not be so uncomfortably close as to risk detection of even minor movement or unnatural sound. With the deer now in sight, success was abruptly thrown in doubt: a covey of grouse burst from the heather in cacophonous flight. An old hind lying on the periphery immediately stood up, alert to possible danger. The decision of this wary hind might well determine whether the day was to end there and then. Minutes passed. She lowered her head but in a few seconds was sure to raise it again in uncertainty. In time, however, she bent to graze, suspicion evidently allayed. Within the group of hinds there was a lying stag. It was difficult to be sure of his size and age but the tops of his antlers bore three-pronged cups suggesting an animal of quality. They turned attention to the stags on the outskirts. These rivals, ever hopeful of nipping in to slake their lust, had been chased out. Three of them were young but a more interesting beast lay partly concealed at a lower level. Its sizeable head was narrow and possibly pointless. A stag with antlers bearing only brow points is termed a switch and a switch is certainly a legitimate target.

They made their cautious approach, inching prone through the heather towards a convenient outcrop from which a shot might be taken at a range of around one hundred yards. They settled into position unsuspected and well-concealed. The rifle was drawn from its cover and a round slipped into the breech. The prospect of success was high but for the fact that both stags were lying. It is possible to kill a lying stag instantaneously with a well-placed neck shot, assuming good visibility, short range and confidence of accuracy, but it is preferable to wait for the stag to rise and in time stand broadside to allow a heart shot. Patience and ever more patience is required when waiting for a stag to rise. Late in the day, should patience expire, devious means, such as mimicry of a roar, may have to be resorted to, with the risk that a shot may have to be taken quickly under less than ideal conditions.

In the solitude of the mountain wilderness, they lay side by side, watching and exchanging whispered observations. The rifle had been slid forward into position in readiness. The silence was broken only by the soft rustle of wind-blown grasses and by the plaintive piping of a Golden Plover. Then they were alerted by a more significant sound: a distant roar resonating from higher ground. Through binoculars the source was located, a large stag travelling steadily towards the hinds immediately below and intermittently issuing his lustful challenge. In response, the master stag rose and was then clearly seen to be a large-bodied animal with a handsome wide head.

The stag advanced slowly, extending his thick neck in a responsive deep-throated bellow, ready to face the approaching rival. As he ran forward the outlying stags were summarily raised.

The one of interest, now on his feet, was indeed a switch. Moreover, his sagging belly and prominent shoulder line told of advanced age. He turned and stood broadside. The rifle came to the shoulder, the safety catch was disengaged and the reticule of the telescopic sight aligned on the target. The light trigger was squeezed.

The boom of the high velocity charge reverberated around the rugged amphitheatre and the sound of impact was perceptible. The stag leapt forward and ran downhill, disappearing from sight. It is characteristic for deer shot through the heart to run for some distance before dropping dead. Confident that the shot had been lethal, they kept still. The deer, though fully aware of being in danger, knew not from whence it came. After a few moments of uncertainty, they took the only safe course and, with noses to the wind, moved off *en masse* to the north and into the distance. Once the deer were out of sight they rose and after a short search, the prongs of antlers were visible above the heather. And, as so often, a majestic animal, strong, wild and free, had fallen victim to man's inventive ingenuity. The cull of an old stag is no more than good management in a deer forest, but deer stalking can be a wistful experience. The satisfaction of an arduous day, a successful stalk and an accurate lethal shot, is tempered by a vague sense of regret. A hunter in tune with nature and the ways of the hill has admiration and respect for his quarry.

The stag, bled and gralloched, was dragged downhill to a convenient bank where it could be loaded on the pony, earlier seen crossing the skyline and now approaching.

In the quiet melancholy of the darkening autumn day, a few snowflakes on the wind stung their cheeks, foretelling that winter was ahead and that yet another season and yet another year were soon to be at an end.

Orton on Song

The Orton estate, which includes the well known Orton beat on the lower Spey, has, I believe, been owned by the Millar family for several generations. I first fished Orton at the invitation of Mrs Millar, the wife of General Jock Millar. The general, who spent most of his military service in the Northwest Frontier, was a fascinating and engaging man with a remarkably gentle demeanour. He once told me that he didn't care for fishing since he disliked "killing things". Perhaps he had had his fill of slaughter amongst the unruly Pathans.

I was privileged to know Mrs Millar more closely. She was an animated, talkative lady and, though then in her eighties, still a keen salmon fisher and capable of wading confidently down a pool. It was a particular pleasure to accept many invitations, either to fish her rod or to fish along with her at Orton. These hugely enjoyable days were regularly productive and were enhanced by the memorable company of the long-standing ghillie, John Tennant. Our friendship endured and, for years after his retirement, any day I was known to be fishing at Orton, I would look out for the distant vision of John, accompanied by his West Highland Terrier, walking up the bank to renew our fellowship with reminiscences of the old days.

Once, seated with Mrs Millar at the hut, I ventured that she would have known the legendary salmon fisherman, John Ashley Cooper. "Oh yes, of course, dear John," she replied, "he often fished here at Orton. I remember one day, I was in the Wood Pool and John was below me in Cairnty." The Wood Pool was a small but productive pool which is sadly now no more having been obliterated by a spate a few years ago. It fed into the large Cairnty Pool, which in past years, when its flow was more confined, was reputed to be one of the finest pools on Spey.

Cairnty at Orton

Mrs Millar continued, "I saw John in a fish. And the next thing I saw was John landing the fish and returning it to the water! I couldn't understand it." (changed days!)

Returning a fish

I went down and asked, 'John, what do you mean? I saw you returning a fish to the water.' 'Ah well,' says he, '"d'you see, it *was* foul hooked (hooked inadvertently on the body) and, after all, I've already had twenty this morning."'

I learned of another remarkable day at Orton when fishing Crathes Castle on the Aberdeenshire Dee. One of the other rods fishing that day was a butcher from the north of England. Standing outside the hut, I mentioned to him that I had just arranged a few days at Orton. He became quite animated, saying that, as a boy, he had often fished at Orton and that on one memorable day they had caught sixty-two fish. The story was that by five o'clock they had caught fifty-eight but the ghillies were keen to continue in the hope of making a final score of sixty, which indeed they did, grassing a total of sixty two.

I was very doubtful about the truth of this story but the next time I was at Orton, I questioned John Tennant, who would have been the ghillie at that time. He answered, "Aye, that's richt enough, but they were spinnin' mind!" Evidently, the fact that spinning (bait fishing with a lure such as a minnow of some kind) had been responsible for the remarkable total apparently did much in John's eyes to diminish its significance as a landmark day in the annals of Orton fishing.

A Memorable Ghillie

One of the most enduring pleasures of salmon fishing is the enjoyment of a favourite ghillie's company. The personalities of ghillies are of course hugely variable. Some are more helpful with insightful advice and assistance than others. Some are keenly sensitive to nature in general and ready to share their observations. And, although the days of the respectful ghillie of the old school, who would never dream of setting foot in the fishermen's hut without a specific invitation, may be long gone, some are inclined to be reserved and reticent while others may be almost obtrusively voluble. But what lives on in my memory, long after past triumphs with monstrous fish or remarkably bountiful days have faded, is the unusually colourful character of some of those worthies. Within that select group there are surely few more entitled to recollection than Jock Allan, a ghillie on Delfur on Spey in bygone days.

During the late 1960s and early1970s, when the charismatic Dr Bob Stephen, a GP in Fochabers, used to take the fishing on Delfur during the first six weeks of the season, I often had the pleasure of fishing that famous beat. By then its former productivity in the spring had waned, but there was always a chance of a fish and it was a memorable experience to fish Delfur's large, attractive and inviting pools. Even more memorable, however, were the ghillies. I remember with pleasure the company of Willie Main, the head ghillie at that time, and of his son Lionel, later a highly regarded ghillie on Castle Grant No.2. However, it was Jock Allan's amusing behaviour and outrageous stories that remain an unforgettable highlight of those days.

At Delfur there were four ghillies allocated to five rods. The head ghillie looked after two rods while the other three rods had a ghillie virtually at their elbow all day. On several occasions Jock and I were together and we had something in common, which may have coloured our relationship: Jock came from Tomintoul and I had spent my boyhood in the neighbouring secluded glen of Avonside, locally known as A'enside.

On one memorable day, having driven up from Aberdeen that morning, I made my way with Jock to the top pool, Sourden. As the rod was being put up, knowing Jock's predilections, I offered him a dram, which received the response, "That's an awfa good idea."

During the rest of the day further refreshment was taken and, in retrospect, I may well have been irresponsibly generous but that was a common and possibly excusable tendency when fishing with Jock. About mid-afternoon, I mentioned that I had half expected a visit from Dr Mike Wynne, a GP in Buckie, whose guest I was that day. Jock's categorical reply was, "Aye, but he'll be doon in the Gordon Arms." And then, "But, when we've feenished we'll ging doon tae the Gordon Arms." The confidence of his prediction was puzzling but the intent behind a proposed visit to the Gordon Arms was perfectly clear. It also left little room for dissent. As the day drew to a close, he told me that he had the old Delfur record books at home, which he rightly thought would be interesting to me. He promised to let me have them on loan when I later drove him home.

As we entered the lounge bar of the Gordon Arms in Fochabers, I was surprised to see that Mike Wynne was in fact there, together with Bob Stephen in his usual good form. Bob immediately saw that Jock was wearing a new bonnet, a deer-stalker of the plain variety without ear flaps. "Michty Jock, ye've gotten a new bonnet. Fit happened to your luggit bonnet?"

"Weel, doctor, I've niver worn it since ma accident."

"Damn it, Jock, I'm sorry to hear you had an accident. I never heard any word of it."

"Ye'll hardly believe it, doctor. Ae day last week, I was wi' a toff, fishin' doon Twa Stanes in a helluva day o' wind an' sleet. The wither was sae coorse an' caul that I haed the lugs o' the bonnet tied doon. Weel, ye ken this, the mannie offered me a dram and I niver heard him!"

The luggit bonnet

Laughter erupted. Once it died down, as might be imagined, good company and high spirits continued until I was finally able to dislodge the well-oiled Jock to drive him home at about nine o'clock. No sooner had he opened the door, than he was met with a voluble torrent of lurid and profane abuse, his wife being unaware that I was immediately at his back. Still undetected, I made my escape into the darkness, abandoning all thought of old record books and leaving Jock to his fate, against which his luggit bonnet would have provided scant protection.

Jock's pithy lament about his 'accident' was highly amusing and characteristic of the man. The small audience of fishermen and the like were entranced. Although the story is now quite well known, I had no reason, on hearing it for the first time, to think it other than original. If so, it is pleasing to conclude that one of Jock's inventive gems has become apocryphal. Of course, should it be possible for an earlier version of the same story to be authenticated, a rather different sequence of events seems inevitable. The implication would be that there had been collusion between Bob and Jock, in rehearsing the scene, always a possibility I suppose, though I should prefer to think otherwise.

The next example of Jock's imagination, though in this case his claim may well have been true, is brief. Once, when we were fishing together, he announced, "Yer faither wis doon here the ither day an' shot a cormorant aff the brig. It floated doon the water but I managed tae purl it in tae the side an' damn't, gin I got haud o' it, it spewed up a sea troot. Weel, I hid it tae ma supper an' it wis richt fine."

I hed it tae ma supper

Finally, Jock's imagination reached an apogee in his account of shooting a roe deer. He began with the question, "Did 'e ken Ned Grant?" I had to reply in the negative. Jock continued, "Ned Grant o' Collie Fairm? Ah weel, Ned an' me wis great pals. We used tae ging sheetin' thegither. I mine ae day we gaed oot to get a roe. But it wis the time o' the war an' ye couldna get the richt cartridges. But, div 'e mine on yon three-heided tackets ye used to get for yer beets? (I remembered them well in regular rows on the soles of tackety boots much coveted by country loons). Weel, I emptied the pellets oot o' twa or three cartridges an' filled them wi' three-heided tackets. Afore lang, I got in aboot a roe stanin' as bonny as ye like. I fired an' I wis sure that I hidna missed it. But the roe didna fa'. I couldna understan' how it wis aye stannin'. But, gin I crept up tae see whit wis adee, michty be here, its lugs wis nailed tee til a strainer post."

The roe that didna fa'

Jock must have known full well that none of his listeners would have been under the most remote misconception that the story could possibly have been true. And, unless the victim of huge self-deception, he could never have believed it himself. Of course, the doctoring of cartridges, exchanging tackets for pellets in this case, rings true enough. I had used a similar dodge myself as a youngster. Thereafter, recognising the penetrative element of tackets (clearly it had to be tackets), Jock's fertile imagination no doubt took off to create the visual imagery upon which his humorous fabrication wholly depended.

A few years ago, on the opening day of the season, I was fishing at Cairnton on the Dee. One of the other rods was a well-known Spey fisherman who fished regularly at Delfur. Enjoying his company at lunchtime and keen to revive fond memories, I spoke to him about Delfur, thinking it an opportunity to recall a few of Jock's memorable stories, as well as perhaps hearing any additional flights of fancy from his unwritten archive. I was literally astonished: the Delfur fisherman had never heard of Jock Allan. The hugely engaging Jock, with his outrageous and original sense of humour that brought fun and laughter to the riverbank in previous years, was evidently no longer spoken of with affection and amusement. His name and memory had apparently been erased. In one's personal annals, memories of a ghillie such as Jock are a significant element in the romance of salmon fishing. Such memories resonate in ones emotions and it was sad to hear that Jock and his stories no longer meant anything to fishermen at Delfur.

Salmon Stalked at Tulchan

Tail of Cragganmore Pool, Tulchan

On 26 May 1978, I was fishing the Cragganmore Pool on Tulchan D, wading from the left bank. In the Wood Pool, which was visible downstream, I saw the splash of what looked like a large fish. Several minutes later, the fish splashed again higher up in the pool and then for a third time in Head of Wood, at the neck of the pool. I took it to be a large running fish and reasoned that it would probably continue upstream into the Cragganmore Pool. If so, it would very likely stop to rest above the tail where the ripple of a large submerged rock indicated a known lie.

I hurried out of the water, down the bank, and waded in lower down into position to cover this lie. The fish showed again in the very tail of Cragganmore below where I anticipated it was likely to pause. After giving the stalked quarry a few minutes to settle in, I made the first cast: the fish, now in the known lie, rose to the fly, breaking the surface, but made no detectable contact. I suspected that the fly had crossed the lie too rapidly and, in order to present it more slowly, I inched more deeply into the pool to cover the fish at a more acute angle.

Stalking the fish

On the next cast the fish took, was hooked and immediately took off for the far bank. The line became drowned and inevitably, as a result, the fish left the pool descending rapidly and far downstream into Head of Wood, the backing well extended. Although uncertain of the negotiable depth of the water, I was determined to follow it whatever the consequences. Down I went, close to the bank under the trees between the two pools, fortunately without being immersed. When I clambered out to regain dry land, the fish was still there in Head of Wood. Now standing comfortably on the bank, I regained pressure, took breath and waved confidently to two companions, Calum MacLeod and Bob Menzies, seated and watching from the opposite bank. Then, when everything appeared well under control, the fly, as was perhaps only too likely, lost its hold and the fish, of around twenty pounds, which had been intently stalked and courageously pursued, made its escape. I did not sense other than an unspoken sentiment of schadenfreude from the seated gentlemen.

On the following morning I was fishing the Wood Pool from the left bank and had already landed a fish of 10lb and a seatrout from Head of Wood. Having concealed these fish under bracken fronds, I continued on down the pool. When I had progressed as far as the Battery (the Battery and Fallen Tree: apparently these descriptive terms for recognised locations in the Wood Pool, are regrettably no longer heard at Tulchan) I saw a distant figure walking down the bank towards me. As he approached, I was surprised and delighted to recognise Colin Evans, a medical friend, whom I had introduced to salmon fishing but hadn't seen for some years. We greeted and amused each other in companionship while I continued casting from the bank.

A confident prediction

As I was coming near to the prominent area of turbulence in relation to submerged rocks in the tail of the pool, I said to my friend that I was about to catch a fish. He didn't give this confident prediction great credence but I insisted on its truth. I confidently guaranteed that I would hook a fish within the next six casts, although I couldn't specify which of the six would be the productive one. As it happened, the third cast fulfilled the bold prophecy and a fish of fourteen pounds was landed.

I don't recall having revealed how this impressive feat was realised, preferring to bask in a new found reputation for salmon fishing prowess of almost mystical quality.

The basis of the prediction was as follows. Late during the previous evening, I was fishing the Tail of Wood from the right bank. The water level was on the high side to be ideal in that the productive area of slacker water above the large ripple lay on the far side of the main flow. Even wading as deeply as possible, it was difficult to cover the critical area without the fly being whipped across it too rapidly. I landed one fish of nine pounds, lost another two after brief encounters and saw another rise without making contact. Obviously, there was a pod of fresh and taking fish in temporary residence in the recognised productive area in relation to (mainly above) the prominent ripple in Tail of Wood. Had I been able to present the fly more attractively, I felt sure of having landed three or four fish. However, I knew that I was to fish the same area from the left bank the following morning and from the left bank the tail could be covered far more effectively. I took a risk, of course, since, although I knew that a number of taking fish were there late on in the previous evening, I couldn't quite guarantee that they would still be tenanting the relevant area the following morning. Nonetheless, had the prediction failed, it would have been quickly forgotten, whereas its fulfilment would certainly make a story worthy of being etched in fishing memories.

Andrew Fowler's Reel

In the late 1960s, through involvement in joint research work, I used to be from time to time in Uppsala in Sweden. During one of these visits, at midsummer, my friend and colleague, Jetmund Engeset, a Norwegian surgeon, was fishing on the Aurland river in Norway. He persuaded me to divert to Aurland for a day or two instead of hastening immediately back to Aberdeen.

The Aurland was predominantly a sea trout river with a run of large sea trout. My brief visit was fascinating: domestic arrangements were tailored specifically to allow fishing at the best times which meant two separate periods of a few hours in bed and meals at times when fishing was less productive. At dawn and dusk, fishing was conventional with downstream wet flies but, during the day, the favoured technique was upstream dry fly. Experts were to be seen keeping a low profile, crouching behind any convenient bushes and casting large bushy flies upstream into quite shallow water at the margins of the main stream. And this technique was certainly successful. Lacking suitable equipment to try it out, I bought locally a cheap, stiff, 8ft long fibreglass rod in a stark white colour. Although garish, it served the immediate purpose. I duly took it home, where it lay unused amongst my collection of redundant rods.

PROPERTY OF
THE LATE
ANDREW FOWLER
£ 5.00

A reel for sale

Years later, when passing Somers tackle shop in Thistle Street, Aberdeen, I saw in the window a tiny reel (some two inches in diameter) similar to a Hardy Perfect, with a for-sale notice: 'Property of the Late Andrew Fowler – £5.' I had fond memories of Andrew Fowler, formerly a well-known surgeon in Aberdeen, having been his house surgeon. I hastened into the shop to secure Andy's old reel, which, apart from its emotional overtones, was clearly a decided bargain.

In time, I thought of combining it with the 8ft rod to make up a tentative sea trout outfit. The stiff rod was suitably matched with a number 8 double taper floating line but the capacity of the reel was far short of accommodating such a bulky line. The solution was to use eighteen yards of floating line spliced on to 10lb breaking strain monofilament nylon as backing. In June in the 1970s, sea trout fishing on Spey was excellent though, in deference to concentration on salmon, it tended to be largely neglected. Nonetheless, I tried the single-handed sea trout combination for the first time on D beat at Tulcan. Using an 8lb leader and a small Silver Stoat's Tail (a tiny tube fly devised and popularised at Park on the Aberdeenshire Dee), I made my way at dusk to the shingle at the neck of the Stream of Cragganmore, which was the unsurpassed pool for sea trout. I had not made many casts before there was a firm take. The fish made a powerful initial downstream run and, limited by the narrow confines of the stream, continued with similar strong downstream runs. With every run, the tiny reel sang out with a high pitched whine, something like an enraged sewing machine at full tilt – a pleasant sound if somewhat alarming in intensity. After a pause in the tail, the fish left the stream to gain the large Cragganmore Pool, immediately below. The bank was clear and there was no obstruction to my following it at speed on shingle and through shallow water during which the length of white floating line was far out of sight. However, the upper hand was gained and presently, through the gathering darkness, I saw the ghillie, David Lawrie, approaching downstream in the distance. I gave him a shout and received an abusive retort questioning any possible need for him to be summoned to net a sea trout. However, he duly put his net in the water and was chastened to lift out a fresh-run salmon of 22lb.

A salmon of 22lb (10kg)!

It had been a memorable encounter during which the unconventional outfit, which proved perfectly up to the task, had been well and truly baptised. But it had still more to offer: I went back to the Stream of Cragganmore and followed up with two sea trout, both weighing 4lb.

A Pearl from Head of Wood

In May 1948, I first fished on the Tulchan D beat of the River Spey. The Tulchan water stretches from near the village of Cromdale, downstream to Ballindalloch. It is divided into four separate beats, A,B,C & D. Of these four beats, D is by far the most attractive. Apart from the terminal March pool that flows alongside the road from Grantown-on-Spey to Knockando, the banks of Tulchan D are tree-lined and secluded.

It was a novelty for a sixteen-year-old to fish on Tulchan D. I had already caught a few salmon on smaller local rivers, A'en (Avon) and Livet, but was little more than a tyro with rather basic equipment. I was directed to the Churchyard, an attractive pool at the top of the beat. Almost within minutes, I failed to hook two fish that rose, one after the other, in an ideal head-and-tail rise. My natural, though lamentable reaction, of immediately striking was at fault. Later on, I was able to control this lapse in technique since I did land two fish lower down in the pool. During that day, I have no memory of having fished or even having admired the long Wood Pool, which in later life was to provide not only all that one could wish for in salmon fishing, but also lifelong cherished memories.

The years passed into adulthood until May of 1974 when I was invited to fish Tulchan D for a week. This gift was given by Calum MacLeod, a prominent physician in Aberdeen, in thanks for my having undertaken his major abdominal surgery. Thereafter, for many years at the end of May, I leased Tulchan D myself. During these years, when salmon were relatively plentiful, I became absorbed by the attractions of The Wood Pool, not only because of its character and productivity but also because of the solitude of its ambience.

The long Wood Pool is divided into a series of sections, the first of which, at the neck of the pool is known as Head of Wood, a name that came to resonate so often throughout my life. Head of Wood was best fished from the right bank. I can still hear in my distant memory the clank of the chain, cast into the boat as it was moored after crossing the river, with the water now shaded from the sun's rays in the stillness of a May evening.

Head of Wood

A short walk down the right bank brought the neck of Head of Wood into sight. The strong current of the neck flowed towards the left bank before fanning out into an expanse, in which the depth progressively diminished to produce an area of remarkably attractive water. Its features I used to refer to as 'poppely', not a term often heard, in which the flow is interrupted by a succession of small waves to create a rippling effect. Poppely water must depend on the size of submerged stones being large enough to interrupt the velocity of the surface flow. The necessary conditions for poppely water are not very often met although they appear to be more common on Spey than on the Aberdeenshire Dee. This type of water, of which Head of Wood was a prime example, may be productive because, as the fly emerges from the main stream, it begins to fish more slowly and more attractively across the poppely area than it would through smoothly flowing water. In addition, the rippling effect of the interrupted current may impart lifelike movement to the fly. Over many years, I came to be enchanted by Head of Wood, which became my ideal and best loved pool of the large number that I had fished. So much so that, in the 1970s, I named our new house Head of Wood, an engaging name that, despite the reservations of my family, has grown in attraction ever since.

At the end of a week's fishing on Tulchan D, I used to be loath to leave the beat for yet another year. Although my companions customarily gathered their rods together late on the Saturday evening, I used to postpone that activity, so that I could revisit the hut on the Sunday morning. I might linger there for an hour or two, admiring the blue spires of the wild lupins and perhaps the secluded flowering of the exquisite heart's ease, both of which graced the river bank.

On one such Sunday morning, the ghillie, accompanied by an aged worthy, whom we had uncharitably christened the gaberlunzie, was sweeping out the hut. As we spoke, I saw in the distance, on the left bank of the Wood Pool, a blazing fire, attended by two figures, visible through a rising cloud of smoke.

A fire on the bank

During these years, the activities of pearlers, evidenced by piles of mussel shells at intervals on the river bank, were common. I was told that the two distant figures were MacMillans, members of a well-known tinker clan, who frequented the river in search of pearls. More significantly, I heard that earlier in the morning they had found a 'good' pearl. The gaberlunzie could see that I was interested and firmly asserted that, should I be inclined to acquire it, not to offer them more than seven pounds. I hastened down the river bank to speak to the two tall young red-haired adults warming themselves at the blazing fire. After a few words of greeting, puzzled by the huge blaze, I asked its purpose, wondering whether it might be in any way necessary for opening the mussels.

"Na, na, sir, it's for drying wir breeks," came the reply. Quite remarkably, they were accustomed to wading the river in normal outdoor shoes and trousers, intermittently warming and drying their clothes at the fire.

"I hear you've found a good pearl today," I ventured.

"Oh aye sir, we hiv that," said the more senior, fumbling in his waistcoat pocket and extracting numerous tiny pearls, amongst which there nestled the pearl in question. Although not very large at some 4 or 5mm in diameter, it was completely round, unblemished and lustrous with a delicate tinge of blue.

"Where did you find it?" I asked.

"In there," said the tinker, pointing to the depths of Head of Wood.

A pearl specifically from Head of Wood immediately captured my imagination. In effect it had become priceless and I decided on relatively modest generosity: "I'll give you ten pounds for it."

"Done sir!" was the immediate reply, as the two of them quickly abandoned their blazing fire as well as any thoughts of continued pearling, taking off down the bank at speed, no doubt bound for the nearest source of liquid refreshment.

The pearl, now nestling in my palm, had been formed in a freshwater mussel attached in a bed, of countless siblings to the submerged rocks in the neck of Head of Wood. In Scottish rivers, the freshwater pearl mussel, which may live to 100 years, is now recognised as an endangered species and since 1998 has been legally protected. Presumably, that has put paid to the activities of the Macmillans and their ilk, whose trademark of small cairns of discarded mussel shells will no longer lend interesting colour to the waterside.

Some forty years ago, on that distant Sunday morning, I had acquired a lustrous pearl, with the significant romantic overtones of having been found in my beloved Head of Wood. Later on it was mounted in a plain gold setting, by George Kite, a jeweller in Aberdeen, to form an attractive ring.

My wife Helen wore it occasionally, although it never seemed to be a particular favourite. Years after my wife's death, the more desirable rings in her jewellery box were dispersed amongst my daughters and granddaughters. But the pearl ring remained unclaimed, if not forlorn, at least out of sight, and hardly ever seen. Now, however, after years of indifference, the pearl ring is about to fulfil a more treasured role, as a consequence of the way in which the story of its acquisition and the significance of its Speyside source captured the sensitivity of a receptive mind.

Over the past thirty years, the land surrounding my home of Head of Wood has been transformed into a much admired woodland garden, in which, during the springtime, countless rhododendrons bloom. As a haven of peace and tranquillity, it played a significant role in the story of the pearl. Quite recently, accepting my compassionate invitation to see the garden, a spiritual being came into it. Somewhat burdened by bereavement, she was comforted amongst the flowers. We sat calmly and sometimes in reflective silence on a low seat. Since a rhododendron garden changes in visual attraction by the week, she returned to visit it several times, with continuing pleasure and peaceful solace. On each visit we sat in contemplation on that same seat. She was comforted and the occasional tearfulness of her more solitary moments, was relieved. With continuing release from the burden of sadness, healing had begun.

My newfound companion was entranced by the house name, Head of Wood. She learned about its source at Tulchan on Spey and it was natural that her awareness of my emotional attachment to the original Head of Wood should respond with sensitivity. She was taken with the pearl ring, when I unearthed it and told her the story of its Sunday morning acquisition. And the pale blue pearl ring, tentatively threaded on to the fourth finger of her right hand, seemed to gain a lustrous and meaningful presence. But she would not accept it, at least not there and then. However, engrossed by its emotive significance, she longed to see the original Head of Wood. We therefore visited Tulchan D in October when, with the fishing season over, the beat was deserted and peaceful. The former ghillie, Brian Milne, with whom it was a pleasure to renew our old comradeship, had lit the fire in the magnificent hut and sat with us, reminiscing on bygone years, as we took our sandwich lunch in comfort.

Then we walked together down the left bank of the Wood Pool and along the wooden walkway to linger reflectively, looking into the depth of the neck of Head of Wood. There, in the shade of the autumn tinted trees, absorbed by tranquillity and the sonorous song of the river, conscious of what that part of Spey meant to me, she saw where the pearl had grown. And the name, Head of Wood was now embraced by kindred compassion, compassion borne of the emotional bonding between two individuals of remarkable compatibility. Now my companion could appreciate what the name Head of Wood encompassed and now she understood the significance of the ring. Sometime in the future, when the time is right, the pearl ring will be hers. It almost seems that it has been waiting all these years to finally come home. I know that when she wears it, as I feel sure she shall, memories of Tulchan and of our emergent companionship will flood her consciousness.

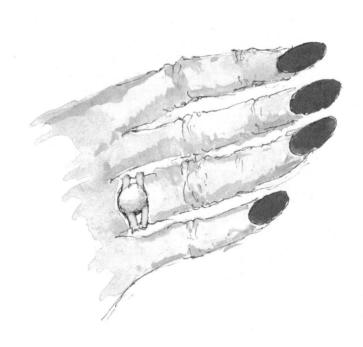

The author on the left with his friend and surgical colleague Jetmund Engeset after a good day on Tulchan D (22 May, 1978).

About the Author

Norman Matheson, a retired surgeon, was captivated by nature from his boyhood in upper Speyside. As a lifelong salmon fisherman he is known throughout the Spey and Aberdeenshire Dee. His extensive writing and illustrative work includes the highly praised A Speyside Odyssey, published in 2019. He was awarded an MBE for voluntary work in the visual arts.